Sneakers
WHERE'S THE SCIENCE HERE?

Sneakers
WHERE'S THE SCIENCE HERE?

VICKI COBB

Photographs by
Michael Gold

Millbrook Press   Minneapolis

For my grandson Jonny Cobb,
who puts miles on his sneakers.

Acknowledgments
The author gratefully acknowledges the assistance of
the following people but takes full responsibility for
the accuracy of the work:
Kristen Sullivan, Sean Murphy, Tim Barr, Paul
Heffernan, Matthew Lefebvre, Elvis Campaña, Gil
Moreau, Hans Peterson, Angel L. Oyola, and Marie
Kiberstis, of New Balance Athletic Shoes, Inc., Bill
McInnis, Jeffery P. Duhamel, Michael Kratochwill, and
Jane M. Cappaert, Ph. D., of Reebok International, Ltd.

The photographer gratefully acknowledges the
following people: Molly Croce; Michael, TJ, and Nicole
Kurek; Theresa and Jacqueline Cordovano; Dr. Scott
M. Pace and Dr. Tracey G. Toback of Toback Podiatry,
Highland, NY; Ben and Jacob Morrison; Shane
Williams; Darien Ellinwood; Teohua Mendoza; Amy L.
Vreeland, Public Relations Manager of New Balance
Athletic Shoe, Inc., Boston, MA; Bata Shoe Museum,
Toronto, Ontario; and Patricia D'alessio.

All photographs courtesy of Michael Gold except
the following: The Bata Shoe Museum, Toronto: p. 7;
© Tom Brakefield/SuperStock: p. 10; © Renee
Lynn/CORBIS: p. 20; © W. Perry Conway/CORBIS:
p. 21; © Anne W. Krause/CORBIS: p. 22;
© Neil Rabinowitz/CORBIS: p. 26; © Earl & Nazima
Kowall/CORBIS: p. 31 (top); © Royalty-Free/CORBIS:
p. 31 (bottom); © Danny Lehman/CORBIS: p. 32;
© Tom Stewart/CORBIS: p. 34.

Millbrook Press
A division of Lerner Publishing Group
241 First Avenue North
Minneapolis, Minnesota 55401 U.S.A.
www.lernerbooks.com

Library of Congress Cataloging-in-Publication Data
Cobb, Vicki.
Sneakers / by Vicki Cobb.
p. cm.—(Where's the science here?)
ISBN-13: 978-0-7613-2772-1 (lib. bdg.: alk. paper)
ISBN-10: 0-7613-2772-X (lib. bdg.: alk. paper)
1. Sneakers—Juvenile literature. I. Title.
TS1017.C62   2006   685'.31—dc22
2004029816

Manufactured in the United States of America
1 2 3 4 5 6 – DP – 11 10 09 08 07 06

Contents

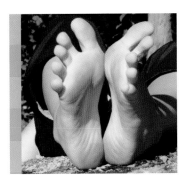

Shoes Go High Tech

When your grandparents were children, sneakers were a simple shoe. The bottom part of the shoe, or the sole, was made of one piece of molded rubber. The top of the shoe, or upper, was made of three pieces of canvas sewn together and laced up. Not much support. Inexpensive. But they lived up to their name. "Sneaks," as they were first called in 1873, let you move so quietly it was easy to sneak up on someone. For almost a hundred years, sneakers were fairly standard in their design and appearance. But that was about to change.

Today's sneakers have come a long way. They are definitely high tech. The uppers can be made of more than forty separate pieces. The soles and heels can contain several different varieties of rubber arranged in layers. They are lightweight and strong. They are designed to make you perform better so that you can jump higher, run faster, and stop and start more quickly, while they also protect you from injury. The uppers can be made of leather, or nylon, or a fabric, called ballistic nylon, used for bullet-proof vests, or a combination of all three. Sneakers for

The British called these early sneakers "plimsols." They were also called "sand shoes" because they were used on the beach.

7

Today, you need an education just to pick a shoe!

running are different from tennis sneakers, or basketball sneakers, or even sneakers for walking. A lot of thought goes into athletic footwear—a fancy term for sneakers. And a lot of science.

Science is a way of knowing through experiments. Sneaker manufacturers have laboratories where they test design ideas and materials for future footwear. They employ scientists who have studied *biomechanics*, the science of how the body moves. How does the foot take the stress of running? How can a shoe help prevent ankle injury when you change direction? What kind of rubber gives a shoe the most mileage? The answers to these questions and more are applied so that your athletic footwear can be *engineered* (designed using science). You would be amazed to see how much science there is in your sneakers. This book tells that story.

Scientists must understand how a body moves in all directions in order to design the most effective sneakers.

The Shoeless Wonder

What if we didn't wear shoes? Some people in the world don't. Often they live in jungles or forests or grasslands where it's warm. The bottoms of their feet become very tough. The skin gets very thick, for protection. Such thick skin is called a *callus*. Calluses form wherever the foot rubs against a surface. If your foot rubs against your shoe, first you get a blister, then you get a callus. If you went barefoot all the time, the bottoms of your feet would become like leather. One of the main purposes of all your footwear is to protect your feet.

Ever notice the feet of apes and monkeys? They are our closest animal relatives. Their feet are more like hands. They can grab things with their feet, and they use both their hands and feet for walking. We share a common ancestor with apes and monkeys. As humans developed, the foot changed when it was used only

The opposing thumb makes it possible to grasp things. Monkeys have opposing thumbs on both hands and feet.

for walking and running. The thumb became the big toe. Its job is to push you forward with each step. It is no longer used for picking things up. But the big toe can still act like a thumb.

See for yourself. Take off the shoe and sock of your favorite foot. If you are right-handed you will also be right-footed. Hold out your favorite hand palm down. Move your thumb in and out. Now try and make the same motion with your great toe. You may have to concentrate on what you're doing. But if you practice, you can do it. Your toe can make

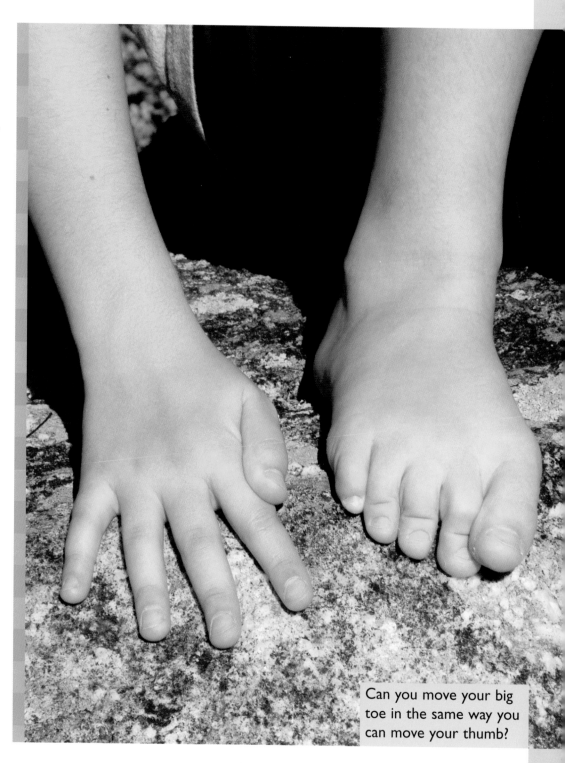

Can you move your big toe in the same way you can move your thumb?

the same movements as your thumb. Can you pick up a pencil with your toes? Some people, who have lost the use of their hands, learn to use their feet to do the same jobs. Of course, people who must use their feet as hands have to be barefoot all the time.

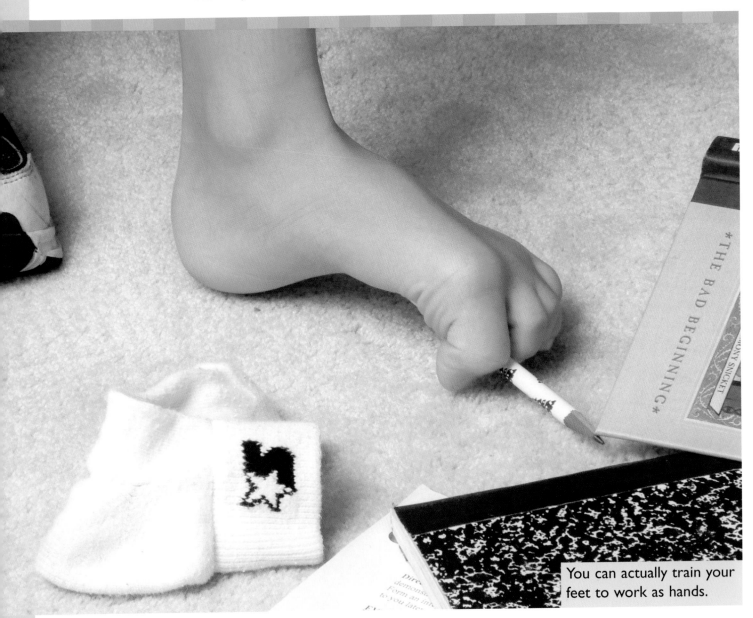

You can actually train your feet to work as hands.

On the Other Hand, There's the Design of Your Feet

Your feet are extraordinary natural wonders. Most animals have four feet to support their body weight. You have only two. So each foot supports half of your body weight when you are standing still. Every step you take, however, adds to the load. During a step, the opposite foot is off the ground so, for a moment, all your weight is on one foot. When you put the lifted foot down, the collision with the ground also increases the force on the foot. So if you weigh 60 pounds (27 kilograms), each step not only puts your full weight on one foot but it briefly doubles the load. That means there's 120 pounds (54 kilograms) of pressure on each foot for every step you take.

Running punishes the feet even more. When you run, each foot hits the ground with a force of up to 300 pounds (135 kilograms). In a soccer game of 10,000 running steps, this pounding adds up to a beating of 3 million pounds (1.35 million kilograms)!

Obviously, your feet can take it. Every day your feet walk or run between 5 and 10 miles (8 and 16 kilometers). (Adults are not as active so they only do about 4 miles [6 kilometers] a day.) So you travel more than 115,000 miles (185,000 kilometers) during your lifetime. That's as if you walked almost four and a half times around the Earth.

Walking and running are not the only moves your feet can do.

Soccer footwork requires quick starts from all different positions, rapid acceleration, instant changes of direction, and quick stops while keeping the ball under control.

They can jump and skip. They can kick a football or stop short on a basketball court. Ballerinas can dance on the points of their toes. The way the foot is constructed lets you do this.

There are twenty-six small bones in each foot. When you take a step, your foot flattens and your bones spread apart. When you lift up your foot, the bones move together again. So your feet are

A ballerina can position her feet to stand "on point" with the help of boxed toe shoes.

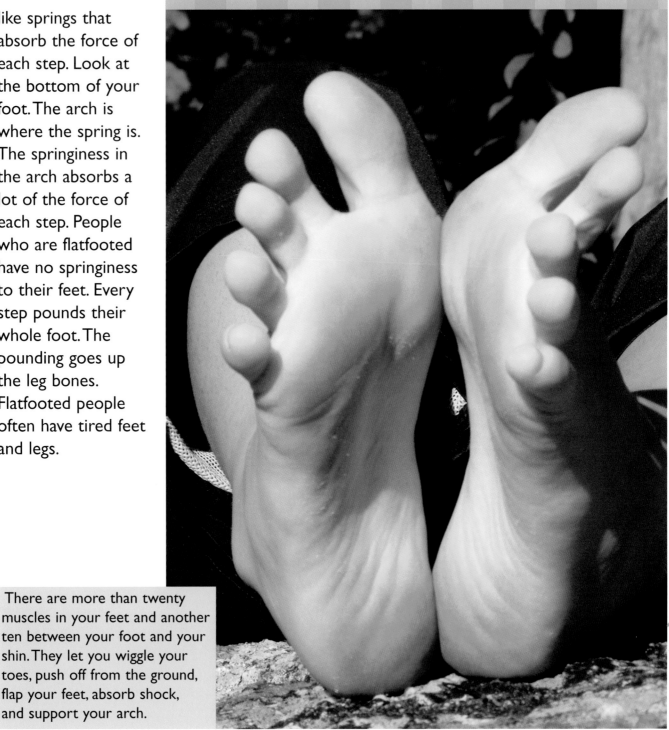

like springs that absorb the force of each step. Look at the bottom of your foot. The arch is where the spring is. The springiness in the arch absorbs a lot of the force of each step. People who are flatfooted have no springiness to their feet. Every step pounds their whole foot. The pounding goes up the leg bones. Flatfooted people often have tired feet and legs.

There are more than twenty muscles in your feet and another ten between your foot and your shin. They let you wiggle your toes, push off from the ground, flap your feet, absorb shock, and support your arch.

Instant Weight Gain (and Loss)

See how a step increases your weight. You might need a friend to help. Step on a bathroom scale. Notice where the needle goes at the moment you step on the scale. The force of the step will register a high number for a fraction of a second, and then it will almost instantly drop back so you can measure your standing weight. Now jump onto the scale. Again notice where the needle goes at first before it drops back down. Running increases the speed with which your feet touch the ground. The faster you run, the harder your feet hit the ground and the stronger the force on each foot.

You, and everyone else in the world, were born with flat feet. Your arches appeared when you were about four years old. Check out the arches of your feet and your friends' feet with the "wet test." Put a little water in the bathtub. Stick a bare foot into the water, then step on a paper towel.

You will leave a clear imprint of your wet foot on the paper. The imprint on the left is that of a flat foot and the one on the right shows a high arch. A high arch can be an advantage, because it absorbs so much of the force of your foot striking the ground. But it may be hard to find comfortable shoes.

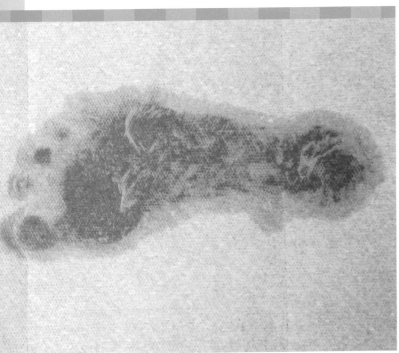

A flat foot takes a pounding.

A well-defined arch is a shock absorber.

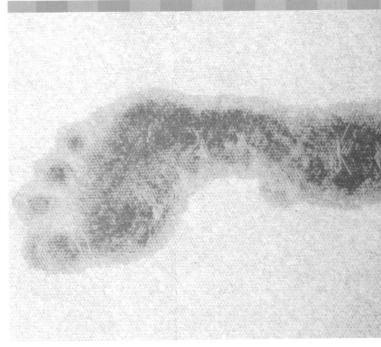

18

Taking Steps

You can see how the foot works by taking a step or two as you read this.

1. The outside edge of your heel strikes the ground. The foot flattens as it rolls forward. Your weight moves toward the inside of your foot. This inward motion is called *pronation*. This part of your step helps your foot adjust to an uneven surface and absorbs the shock of your weight.

2. Your foot is flat on the ground and your weight shifts toward the outside of your foot. You are getting ready to push off.

3. You lift your heel and push off with your big toe. This propels your weight forward.

4. For a brief moment, both feet are in contact with the ground at the same time. The faster you walk, the less time both feet are in contact with the ground. When you run, both feet are never on the ground at the same time.

5. Your leg swings forward. While it is in the air your foot gets into position for the next heel strike.

Your ankle controls how much your foot can move. Check out your range of motion. Point your toe. Now flex your foot in the opposite direction as if your toe is pointing toward your knee. Turn your big toe inward. Now outward. If you move your toe in a circle you can see that your foot has a much smaller range of motion than your hand. (Move your hand in a circle to see how much.) If you land on your foot so that you push it outside your range of motion, you stretch the ligaments. A ligament is a band that connects one bone to another. A strained ligament is a sprain.

See How You Run

When it comes to running, humans are far from being the fastest creatures on Earth. The cheetah is the fastest-running animal on Earth. It has been clocked at more than 70 miles (112 kilometers) per hour. But the cheetah can only sprint for about a minute before stopping to rest and recover. The best runner on Earth is the American pronghorn antelope. It can run at 61 miles (98 kilometers) per hour—faster than the 45 miles (72 kilometers) per hour of a great racehorse—and it can keep it up for more than ten minutes. Scientists have studied the pronghorn to see how

The cheetah is the world's champion sprinter.

The pronghorn antelope is the most efficient runner on Earth.

they do it. Have you ever noticed how your muscles "burn" when you've been running for what seems like a long time? The burn means your muscles are out of oxygen. Pronghorn antelopes are able to get and use more oxygen when they are running than any other animal.

By comparison, the fastest human would come nowhere close in a race with a cheetah or an antelope. The world sprinting record is 10.352 meters per second, or about 23 miles an hour. A marathoner tries to average about 5 miles (8 kilometers) an hour. It seems that in order to be fast, you have to strike the ground hard. This lets runners increase two things needed to be speedy—the length of the stride and how often they take a step (stride frequency).

Trained runners have well-defined leg muscles that help them increase the length of their stride.

Be Your Own Coach

You can make some measurements of your own: To measure your stride, walk or run on a dusty track. A stride is the distance between one toe and the other or one heel and the other. Does the length of your stride change when you run, compared with your walking stride?

Now measure the frequency of your stride. Count the number of steps you make as you travel a measured distance (such as between two telephone poles or a quarter of the way around a track). Have a friend time you as you walk. Does your frequency change between walking and running?

Now have a race with your friend. Do your earlier measurements of stride length and stride frequency predict the winner?

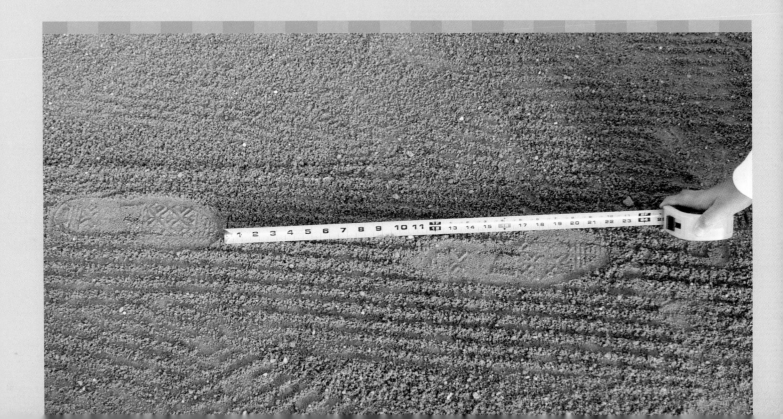

Your well-worn sneakers can also tell you something about how you run. Look at the bottom of an old sneaker. Notice where the tread has worn away. Usually the heel wears down where you strike the ground when you take a step. If your step is too pronated (that is, there is too much weight on the inside of your foot), the inside of the ball of the foot is worn away. A good stride will wear away the center of the ball of the foot. Check the wear patterns on the bottoms of sneakers of your friends and family.

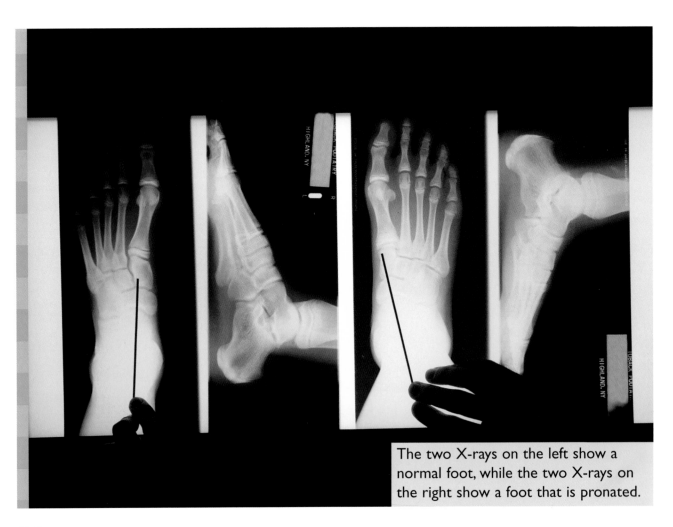

The two X-rays on the left show a normal foot, while the two X-rays on the right show a foot that is pronated.

The top sneaker shows the wear on the inside of the toe of a pronated runner. The bottom sneaker is more evenly worn. The weight is in the center of the sole.

Rubber

The "sneaky" part of sneakers is the soft, bouncy rubber used for the soles. Rubber was discovered by Indians from the West Indies and South America. They made cuts in the trunks of certain trees in their jungles. A sticky white sap oozed out of the cuts. When the sap was wet, it could be shaped or spread on surfaces. When it dried, it turned light brown, it was waterproof, and best of all, it bounced. The Indians made balls out of it. They dipped their feet in bowls of the stuff. When it dried, their rubber "shoes" protected them from insect bites in swampy areas.

Latex is collected drop by drop as it oozes out of a cut in the bark of a rubber tree.

Make Your Own Crepe Rubber

You can see what this natural rubber is like. Paint some rubber cement on a china dish. When it is dry, rub it off. You can roll it up into a ball. It is light brown. This is what natural "crepe" rubber looks like. What happens when you drop your little rubber ball on a hard surface?

Of course, Indians didn't call this stuff "rubber." They had their own name for it. Rubber got its name after Europeans discovered the New World and brought some back home from the West Indies. An English scientist found that this dried, bouncy sap could rub out pencil marks. He called it "India rubber."

Rubber Erasers

Try erasing pencil marks with your little dried-cement ball. Try using rubber bands, balloons, and the bottom of your sneakers as erasers.

Rubber excited the imagination of inventors. They believed that rubber could be used for more than balls and erasers. But there was a problem. If the weather got hot, rubber became soft and sticky. If the weather was cold, it became stiff and could crack. Then, in 1839 an

How Bouncy Is It?

Check out the "bounce-back" of a rubber ball. Tape a column of paper to the wall in a room with an uncarpeted floor. Draw a line 6 feet (1.8 meters) above the ground. Make a mark for each foot below 6 feet. Drop a rubber ball from the 6-foot mark. How high does it bounce? This is the "bounce-back" of the ball. Compare different balls. No ball will ever bounce higher than the 6-foot starting point, but some balls will bounce more than others. It depends on the various materials that are mixed into the ball's rubber, whether or not the ball is hollow, what its core is, and many other factors. Super Balls are especially efficient bouncers.

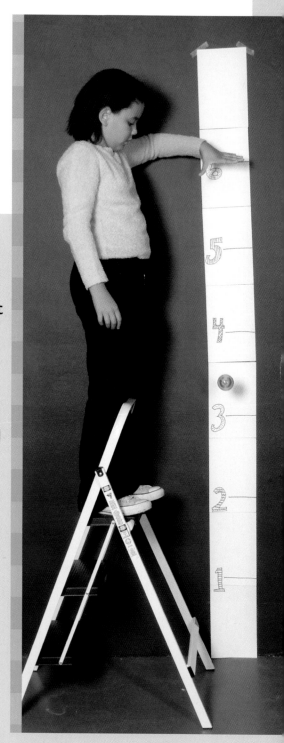

accident solved the problem. Charles Goodyear, an American inventor who had been experimenting with rubber, mixed it with a yellow mineral called sulfur. After the mixture accidentally fell on a stove, he discovered that it became firm and dry and stayed that way no matter what the temperature. Best of all, it still had its bounce. Rubber that has been heated with sulfur is called "cured" rubber.

Since that time scientists have learned enough about rubber to make it from petroleum. Most of the rubber used for sneakers is man-made from petroleum, but it is almost the same as natural rubber. Both raw and man-made rubber must be heated with sulfur in order to be cured.

The rubber soles on the bottom of your sneakers are not made by a sneaker factory. There are factories that make only rubber soles. It's something like making cookies, because the "dough" has to be mixed. Sneaker soles use different combinations of ingredients, depending on their intended sport. A basketball sneaker for a wooden gym floor is different from a running shoe that will be used on the pavement.

The first step in making rubber soles is measuring and mixing the different rubbers and chemicals. Since all of the ingredients are solid, a really powerful "mix master" is used to get them to combine. A giant Banbury mixer at the rubber-sole factory can mix 500 pounds (225 kilograms) of ingredients into a huge, smooth blob.

The next step is rolling out the rubber, just as you would roll out cookie dough. Instead of a rolling

pin, the rubber-sole factory has rolling mills. Huge rollers smooth out the blob into a sheet that is the right thickness for soles.

Next, the rubber sheet is cut into pieces, each with the shape of a sole (or a part of a sole). These shapes are called "biscuits." The biscuits are placed in metal molds

Sheets of latex are hung up to dry as part of the curing process.

that form the exact shape of the sneaker sole with the pattern of the ridges for the bottom design. The biscuits in the molds are now baked in an oven. They melt and fill the molds. The heat cures the rubber. These become the bottoms of your shoes, called "outsoles." There are two important jobs for outsoles—they must grip the surface so that you don't slip, and they must wear well.

The molds are cleaned in preparation for the next batch of biscuits.

Above the outsole is a lightweight cushion called a "midsole." The job of the midsole is to act as a shock absorber. Some midsoles contain a flat cushion filled with air to increase their shock-absorbing power. The material used for a midsole is often a foam rubber. It can't be used as an outsole because it doesn't wear well. But it does make your steps feel bouncier. Inside your sneaker is still another manufactured sole, called an "insole." It is made partly from soft, spongy foam rubber, and it can absorb sweat. Your sneaker soles are so complicated that you may be walking on as many as nine layers!

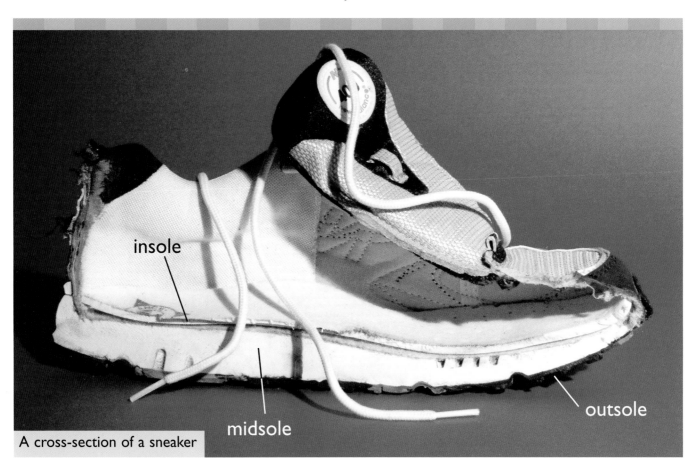

insole

midsole

outsole

A cross-section of a sneaker

Unsneaky Sneakers

Ever notice how noisy sneakers are during a basketball game or a tennis match? The sneaker "squeak" comes from the rubber hitting the surface with great force, just as brakes in a car squeal when applied quickly, or a tire screams during a fast start. The noise comes from the two different materials rubbing together. If the surface is grass or clay or dirt, there is not enough contact to produce a noise. You need a wooden gym floor or a hard court for the sneaker to rub against. Also, you need a sport with a lot of starts and stops and changes of direction. What is the noisiest sport? Design an experiment to check it out.

Stronger, Lighter, Faster

There is no such thing as a perfect sneaker. But sneaker manufacturers think long and hard about making a product as close to perfect as possible. The upper part of the shoe has to fit well so the foot doesn't slide inside the shoe. Laces help adjust the fit of a shoe. A shoe has to move with your foot so you don't get blisters. It can't be too stiff so it doesn't bend as you move, and it can't be too soft or it won't give you support.

Sneakers should be lightweight so your feet don't get tired, and they shouldn't make your feet hot. When you move, your muscles warm up. As the temperature increases, you sweat to cool yourself off. Sweat is another problem that sneaker engineers have to think about. Your feet have about 250,000 sweat glands, which release almost a cup of moisture every day. Insoles are made of sweat-absorbing materials, and the uppers often have many tiny holes so the shoe can "breathe" and the sweat can evaporate.

Athletic shoe manufacturers use a long process to develop each shoe model. First they talk to lots of athletes to find out what they like and don't like in a shoe. They talk to coaches in different sports. Then industrial designers, footwear developers, biomechanical engineers, manufacturing engineers, and other specialists brainstorm to develop designs. If there are new materials on the market that can solve some of the problems, they

Brainstorming at a product development meeting

are discussed at these meetings. How can a shoe improve protection against sprains, give better traction during a basketball game, improve comfort for a long-distance runner?

Next the design engineers come up with designs for the others to review and change. When a design is agreed upon, several sample shoes are built. Usually the manufacturers build enough of these prototypes so they can be tested by both machines and athletes.

For instance, a lab in the research center of an athletic shoe manufacturer might have a force plate near the basket on a half basketball court. As a player leaps up to make a basket, the force plate measures how hard he hits the ground. The force of a jump can be five or six times the

It's important that a basketball sneaker is designed to support the ankle for making jump shots.

weight of the athlete. One of the jobs of a basketball shoe is to support the ankle to prevent sprains, so the developers need to know the exact force on the ankles during a jump.

If you run a mile you might make a thousand foot strikes. Every foot strike wears away a little bit of the outsole. So sneaker engineers have a machine in the lab that imitates a runner's foot strike and tests different kinds of rubber soles for wear and tear. There are machines in the lab that bend materials back and forth thousands of times. If a material is going to wear out, the machine can predict when and how. It can also compare how different materials stand up to wear and tear.

The materials used for sneaker uppers include leather, canvas, and nylon. Leather is made by treating the hides of animals with chemicals. The hide is changed from a soft, perishable material into a tough, long-lasting one.

Mechanical engineers have designed many machines that can spin fibers into a thread and weave or knit threads into cloth. Canvas, a heavy-duty fabric, is made from the fibers of plants, such as cotton. Nylon is a totally man-made fiber using chemicals from petroleum. A nylon thread starts out as a thick liquid. It is piped through a device that looks like a showerhead. As the liquid nylon comes out of the tiny holes, it hardens into fibers that can be twisted into threads. Some sneakers contain ballistic nylon cloth—also used for luggage—because it is waterproof and very tough.

Technical equipment is used in the lab of a sneaker manufacturer to test materials for wear.

One way to understand how a sneaker is made is to take it apart. This, however, is difficult because you need to use a sharp knife. This is something to do with a parent or your teacher.

Only after a sneaker model has passed all tests does it go into production. If you count up all the people who contributed to one pair of shoes, including those involved in the soles and the materials used for the uppers, more than a hundred workers helped make the shoes you wear!

A specially designed sewing machine stitches sneaker parts together.

Workers collect finished
shoes at the end of the day.

The True Test for Your Feet

No sneaker will do anything for your feet unless it fits properly. Your shoes should be comfortable right from the start. Don't think they have to be broken in. Always leave about an inch between your big toe and the tip of the shoe.

The shoe should be wide enough to allow your foot to spread when you put your weight on it. Most of the foot problems of grown-ups come from wearing shoes when they were younger that didn't fit correctly.

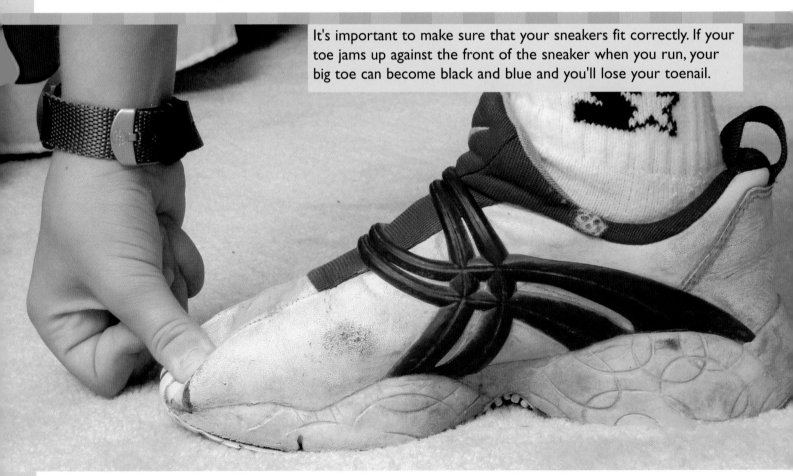

It's important to make sure that your sneakers fit correctly. If your toe jams up against the front of the sneaker when you run, your big toe can become black and blue and you'll lose your toenail.

An Unmatched Pair

Do sneakers really work? There's one final test you can do.

Put a sneaker on one foot and another shoe on the other. It can be a sandal, a sturdy walking shoe, a dress shoe, or even another sneaker. Wear them all day. The shoes will fit and feel different because of the pattern, materials, outsoles, and midsoles. Activities such as running, turning, pivoting, and jumping will produce different feelings for the heel fit and the pressure points on your feet. Some shoes will feel more flexible than others. How do your feet feel at the end of the day? Is one more tired than the other? Is one leg more tired than the other? Is one shoe better than another for particular kinds of movement?

An athlete's mind is usually on winning, not footwork.

If you are an athlete, you are looking for a shoe that is comfortable, that protects your feet from injury, that keeps you from slipping, and that lets you move easily and quickly. Sneaker manufacturers want you to think that their shoes will make you a champion. This is obviously not true, but athletic footwear is extremely important to achieving high performance, as anyone who has played a sport with uncomfortable shoes can tell you. Whether you're trying to win a point, or a race, or just have fun, there's a lot to think about. In the heat of the moment, the last things you want to have on your mind are your feet.

Key Words

To find out more, use your favorite search engine to look up the following terms on the Internet.

athletic footwear	insole
biomechanics	ligament
callus	midsole
Charles Goodyear	outsole
cured rubber	petroleum
flat foot	pronation

Index

Page numbers in *italics* refer to illustrations.

About the Author

Ever since *Science Experiments You Can Eat*, Vicki Cobb has delighted two generations with her scientific and playful look at the world. In the "Where's the Science Here?" series she pays attention to areas kids know are FUN. Take sneakers, for instance. Every year she wears out another pair on the tennis court. That's when she's not writing or talking with students. Visit Vicki at www.vickicobb.com.

About the Photographer

Michael Gold is a commercial photographer who has worked on assignment for some of the most exciting accounts, including *The New York Times*, *Fortune*, *Esquire*, *American Express*, *BMW*, *Mobil*, *Opera News*, and many more. His work includes food, internationally known celebrities, advertising, products, fashion, and corporate photography. He has had nine one-man exhibitions, portfolios published in *Popular Photography Magazine* and *Camera 35 Magazine*, and is included in *LIFE*'s first humor anthology, "LIFE Smiles Back" and "Who Needs Parks?"

DATE DUE

JAN 0 6 2007 WITHDRAWN	
TRDS 3 8 2011	
WITHDRAWN	
WITHDRAWN	